All the Violet Tiaras

Published by 404 Ink Limited
www.404Ink.com
@404Ink

Please note: Some references include URLs which may change or be unavailable
after publication of this book. All references within endnotes were accessible and
accurate as of November 2023 but may experience link rot from there on in.

Editing: Heather McDaid
Typesetting: Laura Jones-Rivera
Proofreading: Heather McDaid & Laura Jones-Rivera
Cover design: Luke Bird
Co-founders and publishers of 404 Ink:
Heather McDaid & Laura Jones-Rivera

Print ISBN: 978-1-912489-84-8
Ebook ISBN: 978-1-912489-85-5

Printed and bound in Great Britain by Clays Ltd, Elcograf S.p.A.

404 Ink acknowledges and is thankful for support from
Creative Scotland in the publication of this title.

LOTTERY FUNDED

All the Violet Tiaras

Queering the Greek Myths

Jean Menzies

Inklings

For Jen Campbell,
who heard me.

Contents

Content note

While generally focusing on the positive, this book does include references to and discussions of homophobia, transphobia, erasure, and other prejudices against LGBTQIA+ folk, including mentions of conversion therapy in chapter two, and misogyny and the alt-right in chapter three. There are also brief mentions of sexual violence when recounting certain myths.

Spoilers

All the Violet Tiaras includes spoilers for the novels and myths featured (if you can spoil a myth). A list of works discussed in depth in each chapter:

Introduction

By the age of thirteen, there were two things I knew with absolute and unwavering certainty: I was bisexual, and I was in love with Greek mythology. Strangely enough, those two things had more in common than you might expect. For me, they were both rather private traits. The former because I feared the judgement and potential ostracism of my peers; the latter because I didn't know anyone else who shared my interests. A child of the nineties and noughties, I attended a pretty bog-standard comprehensive school in Scotland where the term 'Classics' – a subject area traditionally focused on the ancient Greek and Roman worlds, their languages, history, literature, archaeology, and beyond – meant absolutely nothing to me.[1] There was no Latin or Ancient Greek department and my history classes seemed to begin and end with the Highland Clearances (a slight exaggeration but also a pretty good summation of what it felt like to teenage me).

1

Instead of telling my friends how much I fancied Aphrodite, I sat alone in my room reading Margaret Atwood's *Penelopiad*, in which the author imagines Homer's *Odyssey* from the perspective of the hero's wife Penelope, and wishing she would run away with one of her maids (not because Odysseus was a man, but because he was a misogynist). I crushed on the god of war Ares, played by Kevin Smith, and the goddess of love Aphrodite, played by Alexandra Tydings (who, side note, has since come out and become a lesbian icon in her own right), in *Xena: Warrior Princess;* because why should a girl have to choose? And I filled stacks of notebooks from WH Smith with my own stories of Amazon warriors and adventures to the underworld.

Now, decades later, there is something else I unequivocally know: the Venn-diagram of classical myth nerds and those who identify as members of the LGBTQIA+ community has, if not the appearance of a perfect circle, a whole lot of overlap. It turns out that thirteen-year-old me was never as alone as she thought, and nowhere is this more evident than in the ever-expanding sub-genre of classical myth retellings. Whether it be through the retelling of ancient queer love affairs as old as, well, antiquity, or the gender-flipped reimaginings of traditionally heteroromantic tales, classical retellings have become a popular space for modern LGBTQIA+ readers and writers to explore both queer joy and queer struggles.

But why? Why do we continuously gravitate to these stories? Why do we look to the past for something we need in the here and now?

These are questions I have grown only more curious about as I delve deeper into the world of ancient myth. While, like many, I'd briefly come out of and quickly returned back to the closet a number of times by the time I turned eighteen, I had also found the confidence to try my hand at a classical studies degree – lack of secondary classics education be damned. I even went as far as to take on a PhD where I demonstrated the ways in which Athenian orators politicised the mythological sexual assault of women in their speeches, to bolster the image of Athens while othering non-Greeks. Still, I have always been drawn back to where it all began. The retellings. I have been able to watch first-hand over the years as the landscape of classical myth has been transformed by LGBTQIA+ mythology nerds, including myself. Yet, one of the most fascinating parts is that antiquity itself was not exactly the queer haven we might like it to be, or think it is when we read books like *The Song of Achilles* where the love affair of Greek heroes Achilles and Patroclus is celebrated.

Antiquity was rife with restrictions when it came to sexuality and gender expression. They might have looked different from what we are familiar with from living through the twentieth and twenty-first centuries, or growing up wherever you might call home, but they were nevertheless there. Men and women had certain roles they were expected to fulfil within society, and these defined the sexual and romantic freedom that they had (or did not have). Women's sexuality was defined by its usefulness to men, whether as wives or sex workers, and sex between men came with its own social hang-ups including perceptions of penetration as effeminate or uncivilised (although that's not to say it wasn't going on). While I will touch on some of these nuances, this book is not about the history of sexuality or gender in antiquity; these are expansive topics that countless scholars have wrestled with over the centuries. For those who would like to learn more I have included some further reading at the end.[2]

Not only are sexuality and gender in ancient Greece complex topics, Classics as a subject has traditionally been the domain of a conservative elite – not exactly the first the group I think of when I picture LGBTQIA+ activists and allies.

Despite these caveats, however, antiquity also gave us Sappho, the sixth century poetess who wrote of the love between women, and Achilles, the mythological Greek hero who loved a man named Patroclus; Artemis, the virgin goddess of chastity, childbirth, and the hunt, and Tiresias, the mythological prophet who spent time as both a man and a woman – historical and mythological

4

figures within whom queer folk continue to see themselves reflected back. Can our modern concepts of sexuality and gender identity be directly transposed onto the ancient Greeks or their myths as they understood them? You know what, I don't know. The academic in me says of course not, as it implies that concepts of gender and sexuality are fixed. But did queer people not exist in antiquity too? People whose gender and/or sexuality occupied a space outside of the normative, according to both ancient and modern standards? Duh! Of course they did. So, I use the term queer throughout this book to refer to these ancient myths, not to apply these terms to the ancients but to signify how we understand them today, as well as their relevance to modern lives. Because that's what *All the Violet Tiaras* is really about: how thousands of years on from the ancient Greeks themselves, writers have continued to retell these myths with modern audiences and experiences in mind, and how readers have been able to connect with themselves and others through these retellings.

What do I mean by a mythological retelling? So far, I've used the word 'retelling' because it's easy. Nothing more, nothing less. I don't mean to imply that every single work discussed in this book is a straightforward, point by point, repetition of the ancient myths themselves, with a few details changed. Some tow that line, certainly, while others take a more modern approach, and others still are connected to their ancient counterparts simply by names or themes alone. 'Retelling' means many things to many different people. Here it simply means a story, poem, or novel that takes inspiration from or makes conscious allusion to the ancient Greeks and their incredible mythology.

Which brings me to my first history lesson of this book, specifically a brief history of classical mythology retellings. It is important to understand that mythology has always been malleable, open to interpretation, and used by individuals and groups across time to say different things. The ancient Greeks themselves understood their myths as such. A great number of classical myths that have survived from antiquity in fact possess a number of different, if not contradictory, versions within the historical record. Take, for example, the god of love Eros who, according to Hesiod, is a primordial being who came into existence long before the Olympians (Theogony 116*ff*), yet in later sources is the son of the Olympian goddess Aphrodite (see the Eros of Apollonius of Rhodes' *Argonautica*). This can be difficult for those first coming to the subject to wrap their head around, because instinct sometimes compels us to seek out a *definitive* version, as if there is such a thing.

Ancient Greece was not a homogenous society that remained in stasis until the medieval era. Those we now think of as ancient Greeks spanned more than a millennium of history and were made up of various city-states with their own traditions, laws, and senses of identity, whether they be Athenian, Spartan, Corinthian, Theban, Lesbian, or beyond. Naturally, time and place both influenced the way in which myths were represented and interpreted, not to mention the motivations of individual authors and the conventions of different genres.

During the first chapter of my PhD thesis, *The Politicisation of Sexual Assault in 4th Century Athens,* I discuss in part the way in which the myth of Procne and Philomela changes and takes on new meanings over the centuries.[3] Long story short, Procne asks her husband Tereus to bring her sister Philomela to visit them in Thrace. Tereus goes to get Philomela but on their way back he sexually assaults her and cuts out her tongue. Eventually, Procne learns about what Tereus did and she and her sister kill Procne and Tereus' son, Itys, and feed him to his unsuspecting father. All three are subsequently turned into birds by the gods. When the myth of Procne and Philomela is referenced in the work of the fifth century Greek tragedian Aeschylus (as just one example), it is as a vehicle for describing madness, irrationality, and uncivilised behaviour, in which both women are criticised for their actions (*Agamemnon* 1140*ff*, and *Suppliants* 63*ff*). On the flip side, the orator Demosthenes presents these women as admirable examples of Athenian bravery in his public funeral speech a century later (*Funeral*

Speech 28). Two more contrasting interpretations I can't imagine. Sure, a few things had to be changed, added, or pushed to the side for Demosthenes' version to work, including discarding any mention of infanticide, but, because of these changes, and the fourth century Athenian positioning of itself as a state that protected its women from sexual violence, it did work.

Similarly, there are even some (in)famous versions of myths that we can identify a possible origin for. Take the Colchian princess Medea. One of Medea's most notorious myths is when she intentionally kills her own children to punish her unfaithful husband, the Greek hero, Jason. At least, that's how many remember it today. The thing is, until Euripides' tragic play *Medea*, first performed at the Athenian Dionysia festival in 431 BCE, we have no evidence for the existence of this version at all. According to various other ancient sources Medea either mistakenly killed her children or the people of Corinth killed them instead (Pausanias' *Description of Greece* 2.3.10, and Creophylus *fragment 3*). Whether Euripides shocked his audience with the invention of an entirely more viscous version of events or not, there are strikingly conflicting stories of how Medea and Jason's children died that date back to antiquity alone. This does not mean we can attribute any old version of a myth we like to the ancient Greeks, but it does highlight that the myths themselves were never immovable.

Later, the Roman poet Ovid would retell Greek myths of changing form in his *Metamorphoses* (8 CE). Dante's *Divine Comedy* (1321) would imagine Greek heroes like Achilles and Jason trapped in hell. Christine de Pizan would create a fictional city of women including figures such as the warrior Queen Hippolyta, the titan goddess Circe, and the magical princess Medea in *The Book of the City of Ladies* (1405). William Shakespeare would set his romantic tragedy of Troilus and Cressida (1602) during the Trojan War. George Frideric Handel would compose operas inspired by the female warrior Atalanta (1736) and selfless queen Alcestis (1750). Mary Shelley would write a modern Prometheus, as *Frankenstein* (1818) is subtitled. Nikos Kazantzakis would author a sequel to Homer's *Odyssey* almost three millennia after the original (1938). That's not to mention the painters, sculptors, illustrators, filmmakers, choreographers, and numerous other artists who have been inspired by these myths over the millennia.

Every time these myths are retold, whether by fourth century Athenian orators or nineteenth century English novelists, they are simultaneously adapted to meet the needs of that audience, while also demonstrating the timeless experiences that we share with those who came before. In writing this book I have had the chance to talk about its subject matter with some incredible writers and book reviewers, who spend their days enjoying, composing, or talking about these books. In one of those conversations in particular I think some of my own chaotic thoughts on the genre of queer classical myth retellings were perfectly articulated by Bea Fitzgerald (author of *Girl, Goddess, Queen*) who said that 'playwrights and writers in antiquity shift narratives – in creating a queer retelling so too do modern writers, and it's incredible that it is not only the story that connects us but the very act of writing the story that invokes the people who came millennia before us.' This is what I propose we explore and celebrate here: these reimaginings are not really about the ancient world, they are not even about the mythological figures they portray or draw on, they are about the writers and readers today and the communities they represent.

History is not linear, so those requeering the myths today are not necessarily writing something that's never been written before. But right now, in this moment, LGBTQIA+ literature is more mainstream than *I've* ever seen it before, the sub-genre of Greek myth retellings included. There is accessible queer representation on the shelves thanks to the work of countless activists, campaigners, writers, booksellers, publishers, and readers. But why Greek myth retellings? Sure, it could just be that with more queer lit in the mainstream, this will be reflected in every genre. Yet, I still feel like there's more to it.

So, how do I plan on answering my curiosity? What is my methodology, as my PhD supervisors always asked me? Well, I'm going to (over)analyse a bunch of queer literature inspired at least in part by ancient Greek mythology. Instead of aiming for an exhaustive list I've selected a cross-section that, when examined together, provides a snapshot into the power and potential in this literary form. First, a look at not just the timeless nature of myth but the timeless form of poetry and how modern day poets are taking part in a long tradition of preserving human experiences; next, a study of queer retellings which take the myths out of antiquity and locate them in more contemporary settings, proving their modern relevancy to queer lives and how myth grows with its audiences; finally, a discussion of how queer folk have always been here, sometimes forced into the shadows, sometimes – now – finding their stories at the forefront.

This isn't an ancient history book, although there are plenty of references to the past; it is a book about modern queer culture and how the LGBTQIA+ community, my community, has found connection through just one literary form: to the past, to each other – to ourselves.

Chapter 1

New Stories in an Ancient Form

Where would myth be without poetry? Before there were novels filled with sweeping romances, magical fantasy worlds, and mind-boggling futures, there was poetry – epic, didactic, lyric, dramatic, erotic, not all of which are mutually exclusive, the scope of this ancient form is wide and varied. Within those poetic works that have survived written down from antiquity are our earliest examples of Greek mythological narratives. While it is certainly not an art form owned exclusively by classical mythology, it is one that has played an extensive role in the dissemination of these myths over the millennia.

The oldest of these works date back to the archaic era, which roughly spanned the seventh and sixth centuries BCE. Extant mythological works as Homer's epics the *Iliad* and *Odyssey* survive from this period, which chart the heroic journeys of Achilles and Odysseus respectively (both emotionally and geographically); Hesiod's *Theogony* and *Works & Days*, which recount the creation of the universe, the gods, and humankind; Pindar's victory *Odes* sampling a wide variety of myths from the adventures of Bellerophon to Medea; and the *Homeric Hymns* in honour of Greek deities that were definitely not written by Homer. All of which are, of course, poems in one form or another. While we are focused on Greek mythology and therefore ancient Greek poetry, I have to acknowledge the wealth of mythological poetry that dates even further back. From the Ancient Egyptian *Tales of Sinuhe* to the Mesopotamian *Epic of Gilgamesh*, mythology and poetry are infinitely intertwined.

In fact, it's not until the classical era (roughly the fifth and fourth centuries BCE) that we start to see any other literary form dedicated to the adaptation of Greek mythology – I say dedicated because there are historical and philosophical texts which do include brief accounts and references to myths. During this period Ancient Greece saw the introduction of the tragic play, an art form that consisted almost exclusively of mythological narratives rewritten by playwrights and performed in theatres during religious festivals (there is only one tragic play that survives from Ancient Greece that is not an adaptation of a myth: Aeschylus' *Persians* from 472 BCE). These plays offered up new opportunities to explore myths in a public forum where large audiences could come together and experience stories both familiar and altered.

Yet, even with the invention of tragedy and the modern novel still later, Greek mythology continued, and continues, to be adapted in poetic form. I've already mentioned a number of such works, and I could of course continue to add names like the third century BCE bucolic poet Theocritus or the fourth century BCE Quintus Smyrnaeus who wrote a 'sequel' to Homer's *Iliad*, but the ties between poetry and mythology stretch far beyond antiquity. And that includes queer poetry.

The nineteenth/twentieth century Greek poet Constantine Cavafy wrote numerous poems that referenced Greek mythology including those dedicated to his lover: In *He Had Come There to Read* (1924), Cavafy describes the man he admires as embodying Eros, god of love and lust – a two-fold metaphor which refers both to the man's physical appearance in comparison to statues of the beautiful god, and the feelings of erotic desire he elicits from the speaker. Nor is this the only poem where Cavafy compares his lover to the Greek god or Greek statues in general (take for example *I Gazed So Much*).

Poetry, queer identity, and Greek mythology have been inextricably interwoven throughout history. Today, contemporary poets continue to use the structures and themes of Greek myth to navigate contemporary queer experiences. From modern day epics to lyrical rap performances, poets are carrying on an ancient tradition in a modern world.

One contemporary poet and playwright who makes continuous use of Greek mythology in their work is Kae Tempest. From their poetry collection *Brand New Ancients* (2013), which charts the interwoven lives of two modern day families in the style of an ancient epic, to their play *Paradise* (2021), an adaptation of Sophocles' tragedy *Philoctetes* (409 BCE), exploring the timeless realities of war and displacement, Tempest's work demonstrates not just an appreciation of myth itself, but the literary forms through which these stories have been preserved. From this incredible back catalogue, it is their poetry collection *Hold Your Own* (2014) that I wish to discuss in more detail.

The collection is structured around Tempest's modern day interpretation of the Greek myth of Tiresias. According to classical mythology Tiresias, first as a man, came upon two snakes having sex and broke them apart. The goddess Hera was displeased by his actions and 'punished' him by transforming him into a woman. Tiresias then proceeds to live life as a woman for a number of years, acting as a priestess to Hera and a prophet, getting married to a man and having children, until one day she stumbles across two more snakes having sex and ends up back where he started.[4] This transition, from man to woman to man again, remains a defining part of Tiresias' story, one which later makes him uniquely placed in the eyes of the gods to settle a debate between the tumultuous Hera and Zeus: who gains more pleasure from sex, man or woman?

Tempest charts these same events – a contemporary variation upon them – in the opening poem of their collection: *Tiresias,* a longer narrative work in the vein of the ancient epics themselves. We follow Tiresias, 'a boy of fifteen', heading to school when he finds two snakes in the woods... Tiresias the girl 'can't go home, not now' and so she starts a new life, years pass, and she falls in love. When her lover proposes, she decides it's finally time to return home to seek some sense of closure, but instead she wanders through the woods and comes upon two snakes... And Tiresias the man has to start again. Finally 'at peace at last', Tiresias has settled into a quiet life with a new partner, 'a gentle man', taking up pottery and attending the local choir, only to be summoned by the gods to answer Zeus and Hera's question.

Tempest's Tiresias gives the same answer as his ancient counterpart; it is woman, he declares, who derives the most pleasure from sex. Unfortunately for him, Hera does not like this answer and punishes him with blindness, while Zeus' 'rewards' him with the 'gift' of prophecy. Thus, we meet Tiresias the blind prophet of myth at last. Rooted in these four stages of Tiresias' life that unfold within the opening story, the rest of the poems in *Hold Your Own* are split into four sections: *Childhood, Womanhood, Manhood,* and *Blind Prophet.*

No longer necessarily about Tiresias themselves but musings on the constraints, expectations, wonders, and prejudices surrounding gender, age, and love, it is an incredibly powerful collection, where each individual poem manages to punch, but it achieves the most as a whole.

I first read the collection in January 2015. The book itself had been a Christmas gift and, oh, what a gift it was. The emotional reaction I had the first time I read it was visceral – something I can confirm simply from looking back at my Goodreads review, where I apparently wrote that it 'blew me away. I smiled throughout and on occasion I cried.' Now, I'm not quoting myself because I think this was anything close to a significant or particularly insightful review, but to emphasise that I still remember feeling exactly this. Since then, I've read and listened to *Hold Your Own* and the various poems inside countless times, and my reaction has never changed; every time I experience Kae Tempest's words I feel them in my bones.

In the ancient texts, Tiresias is rarely the 'main character', shall we say. They are typically seen as an outsider, a liminal character that represents the other and passes comment from the sidelines looking in. Tempest on the other hand tells Tiresias' story – one which, despite all the fantastical qualities, is distinctly human. Tiresias' time as both man and woman are not just thought experiments, but a lived experience. The pain, the power, the discomfort, the euphoria, it's all felt in the lines of Tempest's poetry. And, as the final lines read: 'Tiresias – you teach us / What it means: to hold your own.'

In an interview with *The Guardian*, Tempest talks about coming out as non-binary and how their art has always been a safe space for them to simultaneously experiment and exist within, noting, 'All this is to say that when I did fixate on lyricism, rapping and music... it was a real lifeline. A balm for the pain when I was confused and unwell.' Day to day, dysphoria was a source of great distress. 'Because I was so different to other people, it would freak them out: who are you? What are you? People didn't understand me. When performing, that was my pass. I didn't need to pass as either gender.'[5]

Tempest's words ring true not only for their own work but the power of poetry and performance throughout the centuries, both for the writer and performer, and readers and audiences alike. This is exactly what *Hold Your Own* offers readers and listeners: the opportunity to explore their own identity, to occupy a space of fluidity and emotional freedom, safe and free of judgement.

The story of Tiresias is an interesting myth for ancient historians attempting to understand how the ancient Greeks conceived of gender, as there existed gendered constructs in antiquity even if they differ in some ways from more modern examples. While some might not like me for saying it, academics don't get a monopoly on the meaning and significance of ancient mythology. Is Tempest's Tiresias trans, gender-fluid, pangender, genderqueer, non-binary, or any of the above? I don't really think this question can be answered, and not just because of the struggle to apply modern labels to ancient figures. The almost limitless possibilities of 'gender' that Tiresias' story offers (symbolically rather than literally) is one of the reasons it has provided such rich material for a wealth of modern writers: from Virginia Woolf's *Orlando* (1928), which follows the three hundred year life of Orlando as they live first as a man then as a woman, to Zeyn Joukhadar's *Tiresias* in *Fit For the Gods* (2023), which recounts a day in the life of its trans protagonist as he is pushed into seeing the future at a wild countryside party. Tiresias' story remains a successful and versatile vehicle to explore, question and understand our own gender identity and what that means to us.

Mythological poetry not only has the potential to explore gender and sexuality, but to affirm and validate them too. This is one of the central themes of *Goddess of the Hunt* by Shelby Eileen (2019) – a collection predominantly inspired by and told from the perspective of the ancient Greek goddess Artemis, a goddess of many things: hunting, girlhood, childbirth, wild animals, the moon, and more. She is also invariably depicted as a 'maiden' or 'virgin' goddess throughout Greek mythology. Importantly, this status as an unmarried woman, who rejects romantic entanglement, is one she chooses for herself. According to the third century BCE poet Callimachus in his *Hymn 3, To Artemis*, the goddess approaches her father Zeus as a child and presents a list of demands. Among other things she asks for a bow and arrow, the mountains, a contingent of companions, and that he let her keep her maidenhood. As such, many modern readers and worshippers read her as asexual and/or aromantic (I'll be using the term 'aroace' from here on).

Through the eyes of Artemis, the collection explores what it is like to exist in a world so obsessed with romantic love and sex when these things don't apply to you. Despite her divine status, Eileen's Artemis makes pronouncements such as 'The only thing keeping them from saying I had it all is my missing love story' and 'They will push me out of history because I am a fighter not a lover'. These lines deliberately play on the all-too-common societal expectation that 'eventually' aroace people will change their mind, that they will meet the 'right' person, or experience the 'right' kind of desire. That there is an intrinsic value tied up in who we love and desire, and that we romantically love or desire at all.

While Eileen's Artemis asks these questions, and highlights these prejudices, there are also countless moments within that combat these expectations. Take the poem in which Artemis talks to her fellow deity Aphrodite. When Artemis asks the other goddess when she will feel 'desire' for another person or find her 'other-half' as she has seen others do, Aphrodite instead responds: 'You are a Goddess, whole, Artemis', and to trust that while romantic love happens to many people, it does not have to happen to her. While this shared moment is unique to Eileen's collection, rather than being drawn from the ancient texts, there is something particularly validating for the goddess of love and lust herself to remind Artemis she is whole as she is, her aroace identity as valid as any other.

It can be reassuring to see our own struggles reflected in the lives and experiences of deities; affirming to think that these seemingly all-powerful beings have perhaps experienced some of the same self-doubt, confusion, and frustration that we mere mortals do on a regular basis. While perhaps a lack of confidence is uncommon among the ancient deities, one thing that defines ancient Greek polytheism is that their gods and goddesses are not benevolent overseers, they experience a range of emotions akin to our own, emotions which often guide their actions (for good or bad).

While Callimachus' Artemis is bold and unwavering, never expressing an ounce of uncertainty, Eileen's shows both sides of the goddess: one who states exactly what she wants, who bows down to no one, not even the king of the gods, but also one who experiences doubt and loneliness, who wonders if others will accept or understand her and who is vulnerable and open. There is a beauty in that vulnerability, one which allows the reader in, to relate and feel understood. As Eileen writes in *Goddess of the Hunt*, 'A lifetime of maidenhood sounds like a fantasy. Sounds like a freedom.'

But it doesn't have to be fantasy. It can, as Artemis has learned, be reality. Eileen's Artemis is a beacon of hope amidst such judgment, pressure and expectations, an immortal goddess who never needs to conform, and a reminder that neither do you.

Artemis is not the only virgin goddess of Greek mythology. Among the Olympians there are in fact three major goddesses known in part for their chastity: Artemis, Athena, and Hestia. In addition to her virginal status, Athena is a goddess of war, good counsel, weaving, crafts, and more. In the *Homeric Hymn to Aphrodite*, specifically Athena is described as shunning all those things associated with Aphrodite, such as love and lust, and instead finding pleasure in war and fighting. Thus, like Artemis, the ancient Athena's priorities are made clear.

While Eileen's goddess provides a vehicle to explore aroace identities, it is not uncommon to see the 'maiden' goddesses reimagined as lesbians by both modern writers and worshippers. This can be seen in the version of Athena, goddess of war, weaving, and wisdom, from

Nikita Gill's *Great Goddesses* (2018), which notes ,'They named her 'virgin' for they could not handle her autonomy in her carnality, her preference.'

There was a lack of explicitly queer women in Greek mythology and scarcity of female-authored texts; ancient Greece was also a patriarchal society that typically conceived of women's sexuality only in how it related to men. Authors like Gill present a modern version of Athena (and other 'maiden' goddesses) whose rejection of romance and sexuality may only have applied to society's expectations for them in that given time i.e. romance with men. Take as another example the first two books in Carly Cane's *The Queer Olympus Goddesses* series: *Artemis and the Dating App* (2020), which follows a modern day Artemis' romance with the nymph Callisto, and *Athena and the College Professor* (2020), in which Athena falls in love with a sexy academic called Magdalena. Like Gill, Cane imagines Athena, as well as Artemis, as lesbians, proposing an alternative reading of their 'virginity' as a rejection of heterosexuality and heterosexuality alone – drawing a parallel between the modern and ancient experience of having your queerness dismissed because it isn't relevant to men.

In terms of Athena's romantic attachments, Gill depicts the goddess grieving the loss of her lover Pallas. According to Greek mythology, Pallas was the titan god of war. He was killed by Athena who rather gruesomely strips his body of its skin to use as armour.[6] In Gill's version, Pallas is a woman and the relationship between her and Athena is a romantic one. While Athena still kills her, it is by mistake and, in her honour, she takes her name as part of her own, declaring that she would never have another love if she couldn't have Pallas. Athena's celibacy is depicted as a response to losing her true love rather than something she chooses for herself from the get go. It is a way for Gill to mesh ancient and modern interpretations together, proposing an alternative explanation.

Reading these poems, they immediately brought to mind r/SapphoAndHerFriend, a subreddit self-defined as 'dedicated to historical and other LGBTQ erasure from academia and other spaces. Mostly humorous but open to serious discussion as well.'[7] If you scroll through, you'll find memes and screenshots galore that feature queer celebrities, fictional characters, and historical figures with their partners, lovers, spouses, and so on, being described as friends, either in jest or, in the case of numerous screenshots, entirely seriously.

This in turn made me think of 'Re-Queering Sappho', by classicist Ella Haselswerdt, who, despite her numerous love poems to men and women, has gone through what you might call some serious academic 'straight-washing' in the past.[8] As Haselswerdt highlights, attempts to argue that the ambiguous language of fragment 31 should be translated as a woman who desires a man and that Sappho should therefore be interpreted as heterosexual, ignores fragments like 94 where there is no ambiguity in the language – where a woman unequivocally desires a woman. Not to mention, the false equivalency of this argument forgets about bisexual, pansexual, and other m-spec identities. Even when confronted with evidence to the contrary, many scholars and enthusiasts have attempted to disregard or downplay romantic and sexual love between women throughout history – this, to me, is what Gill's poems address.

This is not to say that Athena's virginal status is some sort of ancient lesbian erasure. Such a declaration, I would argue, could easily be construed as aroace erasure in itself. In exploring this topic so deeply over the years, one of the things I've had to navigate is balancing my own inter-pretation of a myth or mythical figure against someone else's. I realised pretty early on that choosing sides wasn't the point. After all, I'm not sitting here at my desk, can of Irn Bru in hand, with the intention of convincing you to see a myth the way I do or of one interpretations validity over the other. Is my Athena aromantic? Is my Artemis an asexual lesbian? It really doesn't matter (well, to me it does, but you know what I mean). While we can only base our ancient understanding of their percep-tions upon the evidence we have, plenty of LGBTQIA+ worshippers, devotees, and enthusiasts have been able to identify with both goddesses since. Gill's poetry does not read to me as a declaration of Athena's sexuality, but instead a question: what if? So, what if?

Claiming your own identity as Artemis and Athena do is often easier said than done. It can sometimes be a long and difficult process to learn to love yourself when you've faced discrimination or ostracisation for something so intrinsic to who you are as your gender or sexuality. But it is possible, and this is the story of Geryon in Anne Carson's *The Autobiography of Red* (1998).

Carson's poetry collection/novel in verse (because it is both and neither), is loosely inspired by the mythical figure of Geryon, a three-headed, winged giant/cowherd whose red-coated cattle were famous throughout Greece. Geryon's life we know little about, however, as the episode of myth he features in most often is that which involves his own death. As one of his labours, the hero Heracles is sent to steal the giant's cattle and in doing so kills Geryon using a poisonous arrow.[9] In particular, Carson claims to draw on the fragments of Stesichorus' *Geryoneis,* a sixth century BCE poem recounting the incident from Geryon's perspective.

There is very little of Stesichorus' fragmentary Geryon in Carson's poems, except the treatment of Geryon as the main character. Carson's Geryon is a young man growing up in the twentieth century. We first meet him as an awkward child, one trying to figure out how he fits into the world around him with his monstrous wings that set him apart. We then follow him as he grows into himself, meets Heracles in his teens, experiences first love and first heartbreak, and finally reconnects with Heracles and his new boyfriend when they are adults. Their relationship is a heart-wrenching one, where Heracles takes and Geryon gives, leaving the latter empty and the former oblivious. Geryon himself is aware of this in his older years, as perfectly exemplified in these lines: 'What Geryon was thinking Heracles never asked. In the space between them / developed a dangerous cloud.' Concluding that, 'desire is no light thing.' Indeed, it is not.

Geryon's experiences and emotions are distinctly human and achingly familiar. In discussing her favourite Greek myth retellings, Ellen Jones (author of *Loud and Queer*, @ellen__jones) told me, '*Autobiography of Red* is probably the one that has stuck with me longest. I read it when I was maybe fifteen years old, which was a time when I was being swamped by homophobia.' Ellen, who studied Classics at university like myself, continued, 'I am someone who spends a lot of time dealing with some of the harder, darker aspects that come with being LGBTQ+ in my day to day. When I read these retellings, when I see our narratives woven throughout, I remember that we are not new and we have survived for millennia.'

As a story of heartbreak, queer grief, and fitting in (or, not fitting in), *Autobiography of Red* perfectly straddles these simultaneously darker and more hopeful aspects of the queer experience. Like Ellen and myself, it's interesting to note that Carson is also a classicist, something which surely informs her modern interpretation of myth.

Carson was once asked by Eleanor Watchel in the literary journal *Brick,* what it was about this myth that inspired her modern, queer interpretation. 'Absolutely nothing,' she noted, in what may come as a surprising response. 'In the ancient myth Herakles goes there, confronts Geryon and kills him and the story is over. But in other ancient sources, for example the *Iliad*, there's a certain amount of reference to homoerotic tenderness and it's interesting to me how that works in a story and I wanted to give Geryon a fun part to his life.'[10]

It is both an entirely new story and an incredibly old one. Rather than the tale of a monstrous giant slain by a Greek hero, this is the story of a conflicted young man whose heart is broken by the self-same hero: the death of something else entirely, but no less tied up in Geryon's identity and who he is. While Carson's Geryon may be unfamiliar to the ancient Greeks, even Stesichorus, he is likely greatly familiar to those who have experienced heartache, self-loathing, and queer grief. As nice as it might sound for all queer literature to portray an idealised scenario where love lifts us up, sometimes life doesn't work that way, and it might take another try. That, too, needs to be acknowledged and deserves to be explored. This is not a hopeless story, not when you remember that Geryon finally unfurls his wings in those final lines. What *Autobiography of Red* reminds us of is the importance of loving yourself.

Geryon's journey to love himself is one that, minus the wings, reflects the lived experience of numerous members of the LGBTQIA+ community, one that often starts in childhood. An important part of learning to accept your gender or sexuality in a world still rife with prejudice, however, is being able to see yourself reflected in the media you consume.

The Song of Us by Kate Fussner (2023) is a middle-grade novel in verse; a narrative poem told from the duel-perspectives of thirteen-year-old girls Eden and Olivia. It is inspired by the myth of Orpheus and Eurydice, which follows the divinely gifted musician Orpheus and his quest to save his wife Eurydice. When Eurydice is fatally wounded by a snakebite on their wedding day no less, Orpheus travels to the underworld to beg for her life. While this kind of brazenness wouldn't work for just anyone, Orpheus' musical skill wins over the hearts of the underworld's rulers Hades and Persephone, and they agree to let Eurydice return. On one condition. Orpheus must refrain from turning back to look at Eurydice while she follows him to the world above, or else she will be forced to remain behind forever.[11]

In Fussner's novel, Eden (Eurydice) is the new girl at school, who shows up at Olivia's (Orpheus) small after school poetry club. The two girls quickly develop a romantic connection but for various reasons decide to keep things under-wraps: Eden isn't out yet and Olivia promised her friends she wouldn't do anything to cause drama at poetry club. Rather than a death pulling the two apart as in the original myth, the turning point of the novel is when Eden ditches Olivia to hang out with some other kids at school. In a fit of jealousy, Olivia responds by saying some incredibly cruel things to the girl she is supposed to love. Both girls have their own troubles at home and up until this point their budding relationship had been a safe and joyful lifeline between them, until it dies its own kind of death. Rather than travel to the underworld (or travel at all) to save the girl she loves, Olivia embarks on a symbolic journey to repair the rift between them, reaching across the divide using the thing they first connected over – poetry.

This book has so many layers that Shrek might see himself in its pages. The ancient Orpheus is a musician, a lyricist, who wins over the god and goddess of the underworld with his song. This is paralleled by both girls' interest in poetry, Olivia's interest in playing music, and Eden's strategy to win back her affection. In the vein of

Homer and Apollonius of Rhodes before her, Fussner weaves an epic narrative of courage, struggle, and discovery. One that explores poetry's relationship with myth, myths relationship with human emotions, and our emotional relationship with poetry. It's a love letter to the power of poetry shared through a poem about love itself, and most importantly, queer love.

There is more at stake than teenage romance, as devastating as that can be. While Eden's parents are supportive of their daughter's sexuality, the same cannot be said for Olivia's father. To win Olivia back, Eden arranges a poetry evening at a local cafe, where she plans to publicly read a poem dedicated to her. At first it seems as though Olivia might not show, but as Eden begins her reading, there she is standing in the door. All might be saved, until Olivia's father shows up to drag her away. This is the parallel for Orpheus' mistake in the underworld; Eden's messages alerted Olivia's father to the nature of their relationship. Homophobia at home is Olivia's underworld, and her father perhaps is its ruler, Hades himself.

When speaking to Kate Fussner about this book, her passion for the power of literature and retellings, especially when it comes to young people, shone through.

'It's been a joy to connect with other readers and writers over queer retellings, not only of Greek myths but of other kinds of stories,' she says. 'I think retellings pose such interesting questions around what counts as an adaptation, what makes the core of a story, and what can be shifted to create a nuanced but connected retelling. As a teacher, I taught from a collection of Edgar Allen Poe stories reimagined by modern YA authors, *His Hideous Heart* edited by Dahlia Adler, and it was a delight to discuss with students how pieces of retellings can remain the same while so much of the story can be re-envisioned.'

As someone who went to primary school when Section 28 was still in force (a UK government act that enforced the 'prohibition on promoting homosexuality by teaching or by publishing material'[12]), yet who figured out they were bisexual around the age of twelve, it is incredibly validating to see more LGBTQIA+ representation in books aimed at this age range; books that acknowledge these feelings and experiences in young women, especially in a world that so often tries to paint conversations around gender and sexuality as inappropriate for children and teens.

This has also been equally reflected in my conversation with other authors and readers. Elizabeth Tammi (author of *Outrun the Wind*) talked about one of the Greek myth retellings that most impacted her at as a teen: 'I distinctly remember reading *The House of Hades* (2013) by Rick Riordan as a teenager and being absolutely floored by finding out that the character of Nico di Angelo was gay. At the time, it was such a revolutionary and meaningful reveal to have in such a prominent series aimed at younger readers. It still is revolutionary and meaningful! It was so exciting and affirming to read at a young age myself, and it's been great to see what a validating impact queer fiction has had for readers of all ages over the past decade or so.'

Brynne Rebele-Henry (author of *Orpheus Girl*) also stated, on the current state of LGBTQIA+ representation in Greek myth retellings: 'I am so excited for this generation of teens growing up in a time of expanding representation and queer stories, but simultaneously, with 'Don't Say Gay' and the variety of racist, homophobic, and transphobic legislature being introduced, it's profoundly important to protect youth and their stories.'

It's not that there are no longer threats to the LGBTQIA+ community, but that the continued presence of these attitudes is why the prominence of these retellings is so important.

I know I would have loved to read a story inspired by my favourite myths that reflected my queer identity as a child or teen, something I never got to. (Although I did watch Xena and Gabrielle kiss in *Xena: Warrior Princess* (1995-2001) so I'm still pretty buzzed about that.) While the queering of Greek mythology is not a new phenomenon, the way in which it is being embraced by the mainstream is encouraging in terms of accessibility for readers of all ages. In addition to stories like *The Song of Us* and Rick Riordon's expansive mythological universe, a number of middle grade works that engage more loosely with Greek mythology immediately spring to mind, including but not limited to the *Lumberjanes*, a comic book series by Shannon Watters, Grace Ellis, Gus Allen, and ND Stevenson (2014-2020) that follows a group of girls whose adventures at summer camp include meeting the goddess Artemis, and Dean Atta's novel in verse *Black Flamingo* (2019), a queer coming of age story that features a Barbie version of Aphrodite. Of course, queer literature for children exists outside of Greek mythology retellings, but it is reassuring to see that this phenomena is inclusive of all literary age ranges.

From Tempest to Fussner there is a sense that we are not only connected to the past through the myths we continue to tell but through the form in which we tell them. Poetry has been used by to seamlessly meld queer experiences with Greek mythology, in those books discussed, and many more beyond. Their work bridges the gap between the ancient and the modern through gifting us with this shared experience. As the ancient Greek philosopher Aristotle puts it: 'Poetry speaks universally, while history speaks of particulars.' (*Poetics,* tr. me).

Chapter 2
Still Relevant

There are many ways to tell a story. While prose fiction may not have been the ancient vehicle for these tales, the novel has proven a popular form to adapt them for the modern day. A notable sub-genre within the sub-genre that already is classical myth retellings is the one in which writers take ancient stories of gods and heroes and weave contemporary and futuristic tales. Think *Percy Jackson and the Lightning Thief* by Rick Riordan, where the titular protagonist is the twenty-first century son of Poseidon, or *Home Fire* by Kamila Shamsi, which reimagines the myth of Antigone but with a focus on radicalisation and islamophobia.

Yet the phenomenon of adapting Greek myths in a time period outside of their original setting is not one exclusively reserved for the twenty-first century. Head back to the 1890s and Arthur Machen wrote *The Great*

God Pan (1894), a horror novella that depicts the strange and gruesome deeds of a woman named Helen who turns out to be the child of the Greek god Pan, conceived through an experiment performed on her mother. Then, there are works where the link with Greek mythology is less explicit. While not quite contemporaneous with its author, Toni Morrison's novel *Beloved* (1987), set in the nineteenth century, follows the formerly enslaved Sethe who is haunted by the daughter she killed in an attempt to save them from enslavement. *Beloved* is an incredible novel that can be read and understood without any passing thought to Greek mythology, yet due to its themes of infanticide and motherhood, scholars like Shelley Haley have highlighted the thematic and narrative overlaps between Morrison's books and the myth of Medea, while also discussing how considering them in tandem can help further our understanding of both the novel and the myth. As an example, Haley suggests one way in which *Beloved* can enrich our consideration of Medea is through framing her experiences as a woman of colour – one who is transplanted from her home and treated as an outsider by the Greeks.[13] In many ways, it is a symbiotic relationship.

As we've established, modern writers draw on ancient themes and narratives to explore contemporary experiences, epitomising the timeless nature of these tales. A story that might not appear queer at first glance can still provide parallels for LGBTQIA+ experiences – whether that be queer struggles or queer joy.

A perfect example where this all comes together is the young adult novel *Orpheus Girl* by Brynne Rebele-Henry (2019). *Orpheus Girl* is, unsurprisingly, a loose retelling of the myth of Orpheus and Eurydice. Rebele-Henry's novel follows the narrator Raya, a sixteen-year-old girl living in a conservative Texan town, and her best friend/first love Sarah, the daughter of their local pastor, both of whom are sent to a conversion therapy camp by their families when it is revealed the two are in a romantic relationship – something that continues to be the reality for many.[14] From the outset, Raya shares her personal fascination with Greek mythology, stemming from when she first watched her estranged mother playing the mythological queen of Sparta, Helen, on a television show.

Raya repeatedly draws parallels between mythology, particularly Orpheus and Eurydice, and her situation, a technique she develops as a self-aware coping mechanism within her horrifying circumstances. Rebele-Henry overtly depicts how an individual can find comfort in myth. Processing her experiences through the lens of an ancient story reminds her that she does not struggle alone, while also helping her distance herself from the here and now.

Throughout, Raya explicitly casts herself in the role of Orpheus who has journeyed to the underworld (the conversion camp) to save his (her) great love, Eurydice (Sarah), and return with them both to the world of the living (the world outside the camp). Sarah is sent away first by her parents after both girls are forced out of the closet. Raya is then sent to the same conversion camp the following day by her grandmother who was recommended its facilities by Sarah's parents. Although Raya is devastated that she and Sarah have been rejected by their community and effectively imprisoned in this institution, she is reassured by the fact that she and Sarah will still be together. She sees this as an opportunity for her to save the girl she loves and for them to escape. It is in this moment she first embodies Orpheus.

The only problem with this comparison is that in the myth Orpheus fails. He does not heed Hades' instructions and turns back to look for Eurydice as he is leaving the underworld only to lose her once more thanks to that very action. While this may be a sign of foreboding to readers, Raya appears to ignore this aspect of the story. She could be seen to be in denial, so desperate to find hope anywhere that she frames her life in terms of a mythological story in order to distance herself from what is happening to her and find strength. While Raya is Orpheus, she does not have to be herself.

Beyond the overarching Orpheus and Eurydice

structure, various Greek myths are referenced by Raya, drawing further parallels. Char, an ex 'patient' turned staff member who roams the camp at night thwarting any escape attempts, is compared to the three-headed dog Cerberus who guards the gates to the underworld, preventing those trapped there from returning to the land of the living. Raya also compares herself to Sisyphus, who was cursed to spend eternity in the underworld rolling a stone up a hill only for it to roll back down again each time, when she and the other teens are forced to move rocks as part of their treatment: a physically exhausting and mentally monotonous task meant to break their resolve and bend them to the camp's primary goal, hetero-sexuality and gender conformity.

The function of these myths is twofold. For the reader, it aids in their understanding of Raya's numerous predic-aments and emotions by creating vivid imagery rooted in comparable stories. For Raya, the stories and characters of Greek mythology themselves act as a coping mech-anism for her to deal with her own situation and feelings. Each time Raya uses myth to relate the nature of her situation, she is removing herself from the torment she is forced to undergo by imagining she is part of something ancient.

As both girls go through their 'treatment', Raya plans how she will get Sarah and herself out. As each attempt fails, Raya begins to lose hope and the unfortunate ending of the original myth comes into play. Raya begins to see her story as doomed to a devastating ending much like Orpheus. While in the ancient myth Orpheus fails to save the love of his life, Rebele-Henry shows that future incarnations have the chance to. Their story ends with Raya, Sarah, and two of their peers fleeing the conversion camp, injured but with renewed hope that they can find acceptance in the outside world. As the novel closes, Raya offers a new, less literal interpretation of the Orpheus myth: as she turns away from the conversion camp and the family that sent her there to start a new life with Sarah, she wonders, 'Maybe the myth about Orpheus isn't about losing your love: it's about learning how not to look back.'

Orpheus Girl is a story about identity. Raya uses myth to define herself and her actions. In a world that refuses to accept her identity as queer, as a lesbian, as a girl who loves another girl, she establishes an identity that no one else can take from her in order to survive, to experience both internal and external struggles. Mythology, here, serves as a tool for communication, with ourselves and each other.

If you thought we were done with Orpheus and Eurydice, however, think again. Enter: the comic book *Midnighter and Apollo*, written by Steve Orlando and illustrated by Fernando Blanco (2017). This one-shot, six issue volume follows two vigilante superheroes who feature as part of the wider DC universe: the Midnighter and Apollo (funnily enough).

Both characters first appeared in 1998 and while neither are the first gay character to appear in the DC universe, they were the first same-sex superhero parents and the first same-sex couple to get married on the pages of any mainstream superhero comic at all.[15] Apollo, despite his name, is not the Greek god himself, but a human who has undergone a series of extreme scientific experiments leaving him with a range of superhuman abilities that draw their power from the sun. Similarly, Midnighter's abilities are the result of bioengineering enhancements that imbue him with superhuman strength, fighting capabilities, and healing powers. We follow Midnighter as he journeys to the underworld on a mission to save Apollo who is trapped down there playing a game against its king to win his freedom.

It is no mere coincidence this iconic gay superhero shares a name with an ancient Greek deity. Apollo the god reigns over such things as the sun, music and healing. Within the comic book world, Apollo is a name the superhero chose for himself, something a lot of queer people can appreciate, given the significance of chosen names when it comes to gender affirmation both for oneself and from the outside world.

When first asked why he chose the name he did by Neron, this world's god of death, Apollo answers that he 'named [himself] after a god to give people hope'. A powerful sentiment made all the more emotive by Apollo's accompanying tale of coming out, where he explains that he came out to his family at twelve and was immediately sent away by his father to live with his aunt. After this initial rejection he continues to explain how, after the experiments that give him his superhuman abilities, things only get worse. 'My father suddenly had two reasons to say I wasn't human.' In this moment Apollo's superhuman abilities are equated to his sexuality, not in his own eyes but through those of others. Both make him an outsider, different, but we as readers know better. As bile-inducing as it is to read that Apollo's father sees his son's sexual orientation as inhuman, it is also necessary to better understand who Apollo is and how he understands himself. As he says, 'None of them stopped me. I lived for myself. Not him. Not them. You think you can break me, Neron? People have been trying to break me my entire life.' Not only has Apollo claimed his queer identity through his name but he also demonstrates that the power in his story too. He acknowledges and reclaims his trauma, allowing himself not to be defined by the rejection of his family, but his survival of it.

Yet, Neron is never truly convinced by this explanation, determined that Apollo chose to name himself after a god out of arrogance. Perhaps he is right to be suspicious of the reason he first gives the god. As Apollo later reveals to Midnighter, this was not the real reason he chose his name (or at least not the only one). 'Why do I call myself Apollo? He thought it was power. But it never was. It was the story. Hyacinth. Apollo's lover. He knew Hyacinth was doomed, but refused to let Hades claim him. So he turned him into something better.'

He is referencing the myth in which the Greek god Apollo falls in love with a man named Hyacinthus whom he later kills accidentally when throwing a discus. Distraught, the Greek god either buries Hyacinthus and a new species of flower arises from his grave, or the young man's blood turns into said flower when it spills onto the ground.[16] While Neron had convinced himself that Apollo chose his name out of arrogance, it turns out that this could not have been further from the truth. According to Apollo himself, it is a queer love story, albeit a tragic one, which inspired his choice. It is also significant that Apollo reveals this part of himself to the reader only when no longer trapped in the underworld but safe at home with his lover. Apollo's name is a symbol of love, his identity as a gay man, love for himself, and love for Midnighter, a love so strong that a story not unlike the mythical Orpheus' descent to the underworld arises from it. Love and Greek myth go hand in hand, and in this moment the ancient Apollo and the modern Apollo become one.

All of this is of course framed by the story of Orpheus and Eurydice, which cannot and should not be ignored.

It is interesting to me how many queer myth retellings gravitate to this narrative, one which centres on a seemingly doomed relationship between a man and woman. Take as further examples, Olivier Ducastel and Jacques Martineau's film *Théo et Hugo dans le même bateau* (2016), which follows two men falling in love over the course of one night, and Elyse John's novel *Orphia and Eurydicius* (2024), a gender-flipped version of Orpheus and Eurydice featuring bisexual protagonists. Each time the myth of is retold, it offers new opportunities to explore the myriad of possible outcomes that do not unfold in the ancient version. In the final scene of Ducastel and Martineau's film, Hugo warns Theo that if he turns around he will lose everything but, unlike Orpheus, Theo listens and the film ends on Hugo's line, 'We are moving forward'.[17]

This far more positive ending is also reflected in *Midnighter and Apollo*, *Orpheus Girl*, and, to an extent, *The Song of Us*. While readers familiar with the myth might expect a retelling, queer or otherwise, to have a tragic, hopeless ending, LGBTQIA+ writers are subverting those expectations and reclaiming their joy, asserting their right to love.

But, as is evident, it's not just about the ending, it's about the journey. The appeal is also in the exploration of love, a love so ferocious that it allows one partner to journey into the underworld where no living person should be permitted to go – the same thing we see Midnighter accomplish in his fight to retrieve Apollo and bring him home again. And the fight for love, the right to express that love and revel in it. So, while Apollo provides a link to Apollo's love for Hyacinthus, Midnighter's journey represents the strength of Orpheus' love for Eurydice – two tragic mythological romances that don't have to be as tragic anymore, reclaimed in this modern queer story as they are. *Midnighter and Apollo* reminds readers that the whole story matters, the highs, the lows, and everything in between.

One popular way in which modern authors have navigated writing stories inspired by Greek mythology in a twenty-first century world is by showing their characters explicit interactions with those myths in the modern consciousness.

The YA fantasy duology *This Poison Heart* (2021) and *This Wicked Fate* (2022) by Kaylnn Bayron takes a slightly different approach, one in which myth is no longer a symbolic vehicle through which to articulate contemporary experiences but a literal link to the past in the form of the main characters' family tree. It follows teenage protagonist Briseis and her two mums as they relocate to upstate New York. If that doesn't sound particularly fantastical, bear in mind that Briseis has a magical affinity with plants. Plants have responded to her without prompting since she was a child, but she's never known why. That is, until she inherits her biological mother Selene's family home from her mysterious aunt Circe and discovers she might not be the only one to have these powers.

Despite their names the contemporary characters are not incarnations of the Greek mythological figures, rather – spoiler alert – they are descendants of a mythological figure: Medea. According to the ancient Greeks, Medea was the mythical princess of Colchis, now modern day Georgia (although the mythical kingdom's location is far vaguer than the historical one). Medea was also a follower of the goddess Hecate, most associated with magic, and a magician/sorceress/witch (whatever you want to call her) in her own right. In particular, Medea is often depicted as skilled in potion making, using drugs, *phármakon* in the ancient Greek, to cast her spells, hence Briseis' magical connection with the plant-world in Bayron's books.

Even though Briseis is Medea's descendent rather than the sorceress reborn in a modern setting, there are certain aspects of Medea's own story that appear to play out in Briseis'. Take for example Carter, a descendent of Medea's mythical husband and Greek hero Jason. Carter is Briseis' first friend when she arrives in her new home, he helps her in learning more about her family history, and there is even a brief allusion to the possibility of the two embarking on a romantic relationship made by one of her mothers (although that is quickly quashed by the arrival of the enigmatic Marie). Just like Jason eventually betrays Medea, Carter betrays Briseis. Despite being separated by millennia, both Medea and Briseis are let down and used by the men they trusted and were emotionally invested in.

Meanwhile, Briseis is being raised by two mums in a committed relationship, she herself is queer, expressing romantic interest in multiple genders, and we also meet a number of supporting characters who mention their own same-sex relationships. There is a myriad of queer, in particular sapphic, representation throughout both books. All too often it still feels like LGBTQIA+ characters are sidelined in fantasy stories where their trauma isn't the central theme, as though a book has to be queer for a *reason*; it has to be the central point of the story. To this day I'll never forget the literary agent who, without prompting, during a potential signing meeting for a non-fiction book I was writing, looked me dead in the eye and told me how much he hated 'forced diversity' in SFF as a finale to his speech about how he was one of women's greatest champions in the genre. Because *of course*, diversity is forced if the subject of the story isn't discrimination... *silently barfs*

Bayron mentions, in an interview with *The Bookseller*, that one important aspect of the *This Poison Heart* and *This Wicked Fate* duology is the depiction of 'queer-normative environments'.[18] Simply put, Bayron's story features numerous queer characters because, well, queer people exist. We're here and we're queer and we deserve to see ourselves as casually depicted in fiction as straight folk, and equally cisgendered folk like myself, do everyday. While this point applies to all genres and forms, it's worth re-emphasising in the realm of myth retellings specifically. Not because Greek mythology is absent of queer figures, but because modern versions often aren't. It's a magical coming of age story that will whet the appetite of any history and mythology nerds, and which also just so happens to be queer.

Bayron also describes contemporary fantasy as 'a perfect place to interrogate who has, and who has not, been allowed to take folktales, or fairytales, or specific myths or legends and reimagine them.'[19] This same theme is something that Bayron touches upon within the text of *This Poison Heart* itself. 'Whenever you hear a story about villainous women, you should ask who's telling the story.' She goes on to outline how Medea's tale has been retold countless times by men who seem to revel in her heinous actions without ever querying or exploring what caused it.

Bayron directly engages with this phenomenon of the various mythological traditions surrounding Medea and the death of her children, how she became famous for a filicide she had never previously committed. As Briseis tries to learn more about her biological family's history, she gets in touch with a classicist over email, in the hopes that she can answer some of her questions about the mythical women who seem ever present in her research. One of the things she learns is that Medea may not have been villainess that many of the male-authored texts reported her to be.

As Medea can tell you, who tells a story matters. So, who exactly does get to tell the stories discussed? One of the many things *This Poison Heart* and *This Wicked Heart* achieve is to engage its audience with this question, whether consciously or not. Bayron's duology explores our contemporary links with the mythical past, allowing queer family and joy to intertwine with the wonder of ancient myth, like vines wrapping themselves around a sturdy trellis that was just waiting to be adorned. (Yes, I've got plants on the brain.)

In this instance the person telling the story, whether Briseis or Bayron herself, is able to add a queer, Black, feminist voice to the history of a story that has elsewhere been used to vilify a non-Greek woman. Just as all the authors in this book have added something to the history of each of the myths they've retold.

Contemporary fantasy (or whatever genre superheroes fall into) is not the only speculative genre that engages with Greek mythology. Take *Variation on an Apple* by Yoon Ha Lee (2015), a loose reimagining of the Trojan

War from Paris, the Trojan prince's, perspective which best falls into science fiction. Throughout, there is a sense that the events you follow are taking place in a parallel universe, just one version of the Trojan War, with others, including the original, hinted at throughout the text – a Trojan War multiverse if you will.

The story begins with Paris' invitation to judge which of the three goddesses – Athena, Aphrodite, and Hera – are most beautiful. If you're not familiar with the original myth (sometimes known as the 'Judgement of Paris'), the narrative begins at the wedding of Thetis and Peleus when Eris, goddess of discord, crashes the event. Annoyed at not being formally invited, she throws a golden apple into the crowd, indicating it belongs only to the most beautiful goddess among them. Thanks to some unfortunate spatial symmetry, it is unclear whether the apple belongs to Athena, Aphrodite, or Hera, however, and the three goddess demand a judge decide; thus, Paris is appointed (or Alexander as he's going by at the time). Each goddess is determined to win so they offer up Paris something of a bribe. Athena offers him an unprecedented skill in battle, while Hera offers him the chance to rule over all of Asia and Europe, and finally Aphrodite offers up the fairest mortal woman alive: Helen. Paris chooses Aphrodite thus choosing Helen, who is of course already married. Paris' choice is the moment which marks the beginning of the ten-year Trojan War.[20]

In *Variations on an Apple*, Paris changes this expected course of events; rather than one of the three goddesses who approach him, Paris takes the apple and gives it to the person, or place, he loves the most – Ilion. A physical manifestation of the city of Troy (Ilion being the name the city was known by in ancient Greek), whose gender and physical appearance are both fluid throughout the story. 'Today he was a dark youth, clear-eyed, with curls that always fell just so. Two days ago he had been a tawny girl with long lashes and small, neat hands, the fingernails trimmed slightly too long for comfort. (Paris had the scratches down his back to prove it.)'

In Paris' eyes, Ilion is the most beautiful person he knows, in all possible forms and ways; this is why he gives Ilion the apple. And maybe it's a bit on the nose but when I first read this story it felt as though the author was celebrating the beauty of queer love, gender-fluidity, and nonconformity when Paris chose to give them the golden apple. Paris chose the person he loved despite all the power and prizes offered to him, whom in all their fluidity was more beautiful to him than divinity itself. Yoon Ha Lee challenges our expectations of a well-known story, retold over centuries. The story itself isn't all sunshine and rainbows, war breaks out even without the abduction of Helen, and Ilion falls, but one thing that consistently shines through is Paris' love for Ilion. There is a beauty in that love, a queer love, that surpasses the beauty of the gods.

Continuing on the short story train, I'd like to end this fictional journey with a short story from the queer mythological anthology *Fit for the Gods* (2023), edited by Jenn Northington and S. Zainab Williams: *Pickles for Mrs. Pomme* by Susan Purr. This story takes place in a modern world, following an ordinary day in the life of Mrs Pomme aka Rodie. Rodie (Aphrodite), whose surname Pomme I presume is a reference to the golden apple, has recently moved to Greco Creek with her husband Ari (Ares), who is currently on deployment somewhere unspecified. Throughout the story we encounter further side characters inspired by Greek mythology like Don (Poseidon), Seph (Persephone), and Ducy (Medusa). When we meet her, Rodie is already actively involved in her neighbours' love lives, gifting them with amorous tinctures and potions, the secret ingredient of which are… pickles (naturally). The only problem is, with Ares away, her own sexual frustration is becoming too much to bear.

Interestingly, the Aphrodite of Greek mythology is married to the god of craftsmanship, Hephaestus. It is a reluctant marriage on Aphrodite's part, one arranged by Zeus to placate Hephaestus. Meanwhile, her love affair with Ares is a badly kept secret that becomes all the more public when Hephaestus boobytraps their bed so the two lovers are caught *in flagrante* and heckled by the entire Greek pantheon. In Purr's story, there is no Hephaestus in sight. Aphrodite is living in matrimonial bliss with the god she supposedly preferred. Their marriage is also an open one and it becomes clear that Aphrodite is equally as sexually interested in women as she is with men. Now this is an Aphrodite I can get behind. In fact, I've always wondered why we don't get more explicitly queer depictions of the goddess in modern media. A goddess of romantic and sexual love who does not represent every kind love is not much of a goddess in my opinion. Side note: Rodie also makes a brief reference to her plans to start writing romance novels and now I desperately need a full-length novel about a modern day Aphrodite who is also a romance author.

Now, of course, a goddesses' sexuality or romantic partners does not have to define who she helps (or hinders). While Purr's Aphrodite is explicitly queer, the Aphrodite of Greek mythology, as we understand her through the evidence that survives, is only ever seen romantically and sexually involved with men. This does not mean, however, that she could not represent love other than that between a man and a woman. One need only look to the poems of Sappho, littered with references and dedications to the goddess of love.

In one poem, Sappho pleads with Aphrodite 'don't, I beg you, / cow my heart with grief' (*Dapple Throned Aphrodite* tr. by Mary Barnard). The poem itself portrays a woman in love with another woman, praying to

Aphrodite that her affection might be returned. She begs the goddess to save her from heartache and imagines Aphrodite in turn asking about her about the woman she desires. Elsewhere, in the very poem the title of this book is taken from (*All the Violet Tiaras*), the female narrator, perhaps Sappho herself, talks of the dedications she and her lover made to the goddess of love. In many ways, deities are defined by those who worship them and it is clear that the narrator Sappho perceives Aphrodite's remit as goddess of love to encompass the romantic and/or sexual love between two women. Thus, the ancient Aphrodite does not discriminate when it comes to gender or sexuality (as we understand those concepts today), even if she has no documented interest in women herself. But what if we consider Aphrodite as a literal embodiment of love? If Aphrodite is love, then Purr's love is queer and inclusive and it's beautiful to read.

Pickles for Mrs Pomme is a fun story, a light-hearted, humorous, and, at times, sexy story. It's not a coming out narrative or a tale of forbidden love. It's not about homophobia or transphobia. It's just a story about a woman, or goddess, who likes to spread the love (even if the results are occasionally unexpected). While these are all important stories to tell, it's important to remember that queer literature doesn't have to be about trauma, and in this context, mythology can provide the perfect vehicle through which to explore the joy in being queer. This is, to me, what, Purr's *Mrs Pomme* perfectly demonstrates: the sheer joy.

The range of contemporary works that have drawn on these ancient stories is vast. This is just a snapshot of what is out there, what is possible. Greek myths offer a backdrop for queer narratives, from grief to loneliness, love to self-acceptance, and more beyond. Myths have been providing spaces to explore real world issues and conversations for as long as they have existed, and as these authors have demonstrated, they continue to do so, and will continue to do so for as long as we need them. I for one can't wait to see where queer writers take them next (I'm still waiting on that novel about Aphrodite the queer romance writer).

Chapter 3
Re-queering the Greek Myths

Ancient Greek myth and culture has infiltrated the way in which we talk about queer literature in the twenty-first century, particularly online. *Sapphic* has become one of, if not the, go to term to refer to art which features women who love women, whether they be lesbians, bi-sexual, pansexual, or some whether else on the m-spectrum. The term long predates the invention of social media but it's particularly interesting to me that when looking for a way to signpost books featuring queer women, we have landed on an ancient name. Something similar is happening with the term *Achillean,* which is being used more and more to describe books featuring men who love men (for reference, #SapphicBooks and #AchilleanBooks have over 310 million and 3.6 million results on TikTok respectively, at the time of writing in 2023).

Even when speaking to authors and book reviewers this came up, with Bea Fitzgerald (author of *Girl, Goddess, Queen* and book reviewer @chaosonlympus) noting Sapphic Greek mythology books recommendations are among the most common requests she received. But where do these terms come from? Achilles is a mythological figure probably most famous (in terms of queer relevancy) for his romantic relationship with another man named Patroclus, who we'll discuss in more depth shortly, so let's focus on Sappho for a moment. Sappho is not a figure of mythology, but a writer herself. In the foreword to Mary Barnard's translation of Sappho's work, Dudley Fitts succinctly summarises what we know about Sappho: she is a 'lyricist' and she is 'greek', 'the rest is speculation'. She is one of very, very few ancient women writers we have any surviving texts from and included in those texts are love poems to both men and women. We don't actually know Sappho's sexuality but, given her unique role in history, over the centuries her name has become synonymous with women who love women. Note, when I say we don't know Sappho's sexuality, I'm not trying to be a killjoy and nor do I think that lack of knowledge invalidates the impact her legacy has had on the queer community and for queer women in particular. Personally, I think of her as a bi-con, but then I'm biased.

This is a particularly interesting topic given the lack of explicitly 'Sapphic' women in classical mythology itself. In contrast with the expectation that sexual relationships would be formed between two men in ancient Greece (with the caveat that only heterosexual marriage was legal), relationships between two women were not condoned. Women's sexuality was tightly controlled according to how it benefitted men, in what was an aggressively patriarchal society. Despite this, we know through a combination of common sense and the surviving poetry of Sappho herself, that queer women did exist. And, though they were pushed into the shadows, or completely ignored in their time, many queer relationships are now not only having a light shone on them by authors, those that did exist or that could have been, but are sitting at the forefront of literary culture.

Madeline Miller's bestselling novel *The Song Achilles* (2012) recounts the love story of the Greek heroes Achilles and Patroclus. According to ancient Greek mythology Achilles and Patroclus were both warriors who knew each other from childhood and fought on the side of the Achaeans (Greeks) during the Trojan War. When Achilles perceives his general Agamemnon of dishonouring him, he refuses to continue fighting. Patroclus then dons Achilles' armour and wears it into battle, which results in his death at the hands of the Trojan prince Hector. Upon learning of Patroclus' fate Achilles is overwhelmed by grief and anger, returning to the fight to avenge him.

Miller's novel generally follows the ancient myth's series of events; she begins the story during Achilles and Patroclus childhood, charting the development of their relationship, and subsequently the romantic aspect, over the years, before their infamous ending.

At the time of writing, #TheSongOfAchilles, #TSOA and #SongOfAchilles have racked up more than 650 million views collectively on TikTok, with a plethora of related and misspelled hashtags receiving numbers in the hundreds of thousands. The same hashtags have been used no less than 194,000 times on Instagram, with thousands of written works under *The Song of Achilles* umbrella on Archive of Our Own, the fanfiction site. In 2021, nearly ten years after its original publication, *The Song of Achilles* was back on the New York Times bestseller list, thanks almost entirely to TikTok hype. As someone who has spent more than ten years of their life making bookish content online, first on YouTube and then pretty much everywhere else, I've always understood the power of online fandoms. TikTok has been something else. It has had an international influence on book sales that we've never seen before and whether you think 'their' taste is highbrow enough for you or not, that impact is kind of incredible – to this author and reader, at least. The fact that so many of the books reaching new heights feature positive queer representation therefore is even more exhilarating.

But the question on everyone's lips: were the ancient Achilles and Patroclus romantically involved? It depends who you ask. The nature of their relationship is a controversial one both in fandom and academic spaces. The earliest surviving version of their story comes to us via Homer's epic poem the *Iliad*, set over the course of Achilles' final days during the Trojan War. Here, there is nothing to explicitly indicate they are lovers. Achilles loves Patroclus as is clearly indicated by his grief over his death, and you could certainly read that as romantic love, many have. But, as others have pointed out, the text is far from conclusive and what might sound like a romantic expression of emotion to modern readers can't be definitively read as such for a historical civilisation where social *mores* were not our own. A few hundred years later, by the classical period, there writers who explicitly reference the romantic relationship between the two. Plato, for example, specifically refers to Patroclus as Achilles' lover on a number of occasions in his *Symposium*, as well as specifying that Achilles chose death in part to be reunited with Patroclus in the underworld (179e-180b). So, who's right? Well, I've never been convinced that one text is a more accurate version of a myth by virtue of its age – haven't I been going on about the malleability of myth? There were clearly ancient Greek versions of Achilles and Patroclus relationship that were romantic, and there were ancient people who read their dynamic as lovers. Just as Miller has.

Miller is not the first nor the last modern writer to explore the romantic and sexual nature of Achilles and Patroclus' relationship through fiction, however. Both *The Song of Troy* by Colleen McCullough (1998) and the BBC mini-series *Troy: Fall of a City* (2018) include the romantic relationship between the two heroes in their depictions of the ancient conflict. Meanwhile *Wicked Beauty* by Katee Robert (2022), a contemporary romance novel featuring characters loosely inspired by Greek mythology, features Achilles, Patroclus, and, straying from the original, Helen in an empowering polyamorous relationship. On the contrary, *Troy* (2004), one of the highest grossing films of that year, featuring the legendary hero in the form of Brad Pitt, distinctly lacked the queer elements of Achilles' story.[21] Yet if you go online, the number of quotes, fan art pieces, and video edits that centre on the love affair between Achilles and Patroclus is astounding, many of them citing Miller's novel as inspiration. Love it, hate it, or be entirely indifferent to it – *The Song of Achilles'* impact on modern perceptions of this myth is undeniable. It is making queer mythology more visible, while connecting readers on unprecedented levels to the past.

What interests me most is not the ancient, however, but the modern. Unsurprisingly perhaps, *The Song of Achilles* came up frequently in my conversations with authors and book reviewers about queer myth retellings.

Ellen Jones told me that *The Song of Achilles* was 'probably the first time I saw a queer and Greek myth in a mainstream section and it definitely paved the way for more mainstream representations of classics outside of the confines of 'historical fiction'.'

In particular, it was the story that book reviewer Jordan Atkinn (@jordslibrary) very graciously shared that stood out the most: 'The first conversation I had with my now-boyfriend of two years was actually about our shared love for *The Song of Achilles*. Our mutual love for the book made for an easy ice breaker conversation on our first date and is what I honestly believe made the date such a success. We now have a tradition that when we see a new edition of the book in a shop, we need to buy the other it as a present.'

I don't know about you, but I can't think of a more wonderful example of the potential for real world connection that exists in the pages of a book. As Miller writes, 'In the darkness, two shadows, reaching through the hopeless, heavy dusk. Their hands meet, and light spills in a flood like a hundred golden urns pouring out of the sun.' Even in death, *The Song of Achilles* provides readers with a timeless, never-ending, transcendent love story between two men that I think a lot of us queer folk really need.

While Achilles has become a relatively popular figure in online spaces, there's another queer hero who hasn't (yet) received quite the same reception. *Herc* by Phoenicia Rogerson (2023) retells the life of the legendary hero Hercules or Heracles, son of the lightning god Zeus and the mortal woman Alcmene.

(Side note: Did you know that Hercules is the hero's Roman name? In ancient Greece he was known as Herakles/Heracles, yet, despite his countless book and film appearances often being set in Greece, and otherwise using the Greek names for gods, goddesses, and other figures, he is almost exclusively referred to as Hercules in popular media. Based on title alone you'd be forgiven for assuming Rogerson's *Herc* also takes this route. Between nicknames like Herc and even H throughout the novel, the author deliberately plays on these inconsistent naming conventions throughout history, cemented when a stranger asks, 'You're that Heracles fellow, aren't you?' only to find himself corrected by the hero's nephew: 'Hercules, sire,… it's not the man's fault he didn't know how much my uncle hated his given name.' So, for the sake of consistency and everyone's sanity, 'Herc' he will be for the remainder of this discussion.)

Over the course of the novel, Herc's story is told from the perspective of the various people he encounters throughout his life, from his twin brother Iphicles to his cousin Eurystheus, from his first wife Megara to his lover Hylas, and many more in-between. Rogerson weaves together as many of the mythological incidents involving the hero as physically possible to chart his life from start to end in a way that ancient texts rarely do. Yet, we never hear from Herc directly, and any version of his inner thoughts are interpretations from those around him. In many ways it doesn't really feel like Herc's story. It's the story of numerous mythological figures, some of whom, but not all (I'm looking at you Jason and Theseus), are more often thought of as side characters in the story of Herc.

Now, I don't have any definitive proof of this, but Herc must be one of the most well-known figures of Greek mythology. He must. Whether or not you've read Euripides' *Herakles* (c.416 BCE) or Apollonius of Rhodes' *Argonautica* (third cen. BCE), you've probably met at least one or two incarnations of the legendary hero. From Arnold Schwarzenneger (1970) to Dwayne 'The Rock' Johnson (2014), the hero has starred in countless onscreen adaptations and been embodied by some of the biggest names of their times. His titular Disney debut (1997) has one of the best soundtracks ever composed (citation: me), and he's appeared as a character in both DC and Marvel universes (obviously the sign of true pop culture dominance). So, when asked 'Why Hercules?' in an interview for *Starburst Magazine*, Rogerson's answer may come as no surprise. 'Because he's Hercules. He's the first hero I could ever name, and there's just so much about him in the Greek myths. Even now, there are stories about him that surprise me. The character just goes deeper and deeper, and I love unravelling that mystery.'[22]

While his legend proceeds him, one aspect of Herc's story that often seems forgotten, or deliberately erased, are his numerous relationships with not just women, but men. Like many '90s kids (I assume), I grew up watching *Hercules: The Legendary Journeys* (1995-1999) on Channel 5, and swooning over Meg's solo number from Disney's *Hercules*. Herc was an ever-present part of my childhood, but never in a million years did I think he was anything but straight, straight, straight. There were literally two whole Hollywood films inspired by the hero released the same year in 2014, *Hercules* and *The Legend of Hercules*, yet neither were even vaguely queer. As I like to continually remind people, history isn't linear, and it often seems the ancient Herc is far more queer than his twentieth and twenty-first century counterparts. Well, not if Phoenicia Rogerson has anything to do with it.

We witness Herc's romantic and sexual encounters with a number of the men and women we have recorded as his lovers, hearing from them directly about their relationship with the hero. We hear, for example, from Hylas who, in Rogerson's book, Herc meets as a teen when forced to live away from home and work for a year. Hylas tells of how he feels for the rough goatherd only to be parted from him for many years. Despite this,

Hylas continues to appear throughout the book, as he is reunited with Herc, travels aboard the Argo with the hero, and eventually finds himself in the underworld watching Herc completes his labours. Hylas gives an insight into Herc's life from the perspective of someone who loves him, who is loved by him, but is oftentimes let down by him too. Because Rogerson's Herc isn't perfect, he's not even *really* a 'good guy', he's violent, unpredictable, and arrogant, all personality traits that can easily be traced back to the ancient myths themselves. But, he's still a hero. And in the same vein, he's still queer. Queer representation doesn't have to be perfect. In re-queering the famous figures, in all their complexities and without characterising their sexuality or gender, authors are undoing some of the straight-washing that has been persisted over centuries.

Rogerson explicitly engages in this conversation within the text; not just in her depiction of Herc's numerous love affairs but in the way that other characters speak about these relationships. In a chapter told from the perspective of Deiphobus, a doctor who appears to be of Rogerson's own creation rather than based on the mythical Trojan prince, we learn that Herc has killed his lover Iphitus. The incident was, according to his nephew Iolaus at least, the result of a fit of madness spurred on by the goddess Hera, not unlike that which caused the death of his first wife Megara. Beyond the initial madness, Herc has been struck by an unknown illness, which is the reason Iolaus has brought him to the doctor in the first place. While they are there Herc moans Iphitus' name aloud, which prompts Deiphobus to ask Iolaus, 'Who is Iphitus?', to which younger man answers, 'He is, I mean, he was a friend of my uncle's?' The word 'friend' does not go unnoticed by Deiphobus, as I'm sure it did not to you either, who promptly follows up with, 'What do you mean by *friend*?' What indeed? The same question has been asked time and time again of those writing about history (hi, r/sapphoandherfriend). Finally, Iolaus clarifies that 'they were companions. Close companions. I think they were having sex.' Something we as readers knew all along.

There is also a wider significance to Rogerson's work and works that portray queer men of ancient myth as queer in general – one that can, directly or indirectly, combat modern day homophobic and sexist rhetoric. In the twenty-first century it is strikingly common to see figures from ancient Greek (and Roman) myth and history appropriated by alt-right groups and individuals. You'll find that examples from ancient Greece, and ancient Rome, are often used to validate the misogynistic and patriarchal world views of these groups online – a world view that includes a toxic ideal of masculinity that is anything but inclusive of queer men.

Donna Zuckerberg's *Not All Dead White Men: Classics and Misogyny in the Digital Age* (2019), while at its core a book about misogyny, touches on the way homophobia can be part and parcel with these groups' ideologies. 'A nuanced view of sexuality and gender expression is anathema to them: the only accepted modes of self-presentation are "heterosexual masculine man" and "heterosexual feminine woman." Divergence from either of these norms, however slight, constitutes perversion. The Red Pill community disdains unfeminine women, and when it comes to men, all deviations – being gay, or trans, or beta, or a stay-at-home father – are perceived as a shift toward increasing feminisation (that is, being a "mangina").'[23]

Zuckerberg notes that 'accusations of homosexuality are commonly used as insults on game message boards.'[24] I don't need to tell you that there exists a strong sense of homophobia and transphobia among such communities, but these are also the same people posting pictures of the Trojan prince Hector with the words 'Protect. Provide. Procreate. This is what peak masculinity looks like' online in support of 'traditional' gender roles.[25] They are the same people producing posters featuring Hercules that read 'Protect Your Heritage' as part of wider white-supremacist campaigns on college campuses.[26] And they are the same people including pictures of Brad Pitt's Achilles in a bizarre anti-LGBTQIA+ video supposed to depict the ideal man posted on behalf of US politician Ron DeSantis. These are the same people adopting images from Greek mythology in order to promote their own political ideologies despite the fact that Greek myth also features one of the very things they are so set against: homosexuality.

While there is plenty about antiquity I would not wish to resurrect, many of the men these groups admire were, as we have seen, having sex with other men – something these groups outrightly deride. Maybe the countless decades of pop-culture 'straight-washing' have made us forget this, and emboldened those who would appropriate these myths. Despite all of this, I was reassured to read about the response Rogerson's book received in her *Starburst* interview. 'It's something I worried about a lot when I was writing and querying, that there would be clap-back about the idea of a queer Hercules, but I've experienced some incredible support and enthusiasm about it. I'm really thankful for everyone before me who's made that the landscape I'm working in today.'

To portray Herc in all his queer glory is in itself an important and radical act. He, like many other mythical figures, has been straight-washed, his image adopted and repurposed by homophobic groups in the real world, but the space being carved – craved – to retell these stories with their queer origins offers us something special. It's something that we can all hope to see happen more often in the future.

You may have gathered by now that ancient Greece was a patriarchal society, and this informed the treatment of women's sexuality as much, albeit differently, than men's. While a story about a queer Heracles reclaims an existing narrative that certain audiences have attempted to erase, stories about queer women expand upon their mythological counterparts to make space for those who do not have a voice in the ancient texts. Take, *Outrun the Wind* (2018), the debut Young Adult novel by Elizabeth Tammi, as an example.

Outrun the Wind is told through the dual perspectives of Atalanta, the ancient heroine of Greek mythology, and Kahina, a fictionalised huntress of Artemis created by the author. According to Greek mythology Atalanta was abandoned by her father, the King of Arcadia, as a baby, for the simple crime of being born a girl. Luckily for her though, she was nursed by a mother bear and eventually taken in by hunters who taught her all they knew. She spends her early years proving her skills as a warrior only for her reputation to spread and for her father (the one who ditched her) to finally seek her out. When reinstated as the princess of Arcadia, she is told she must take a husband, something she has thus far refused. One thing leads to another and after a racing contest and a lot of divinely assisted cheating, Atalanta ends up married to a man named Hippomenes.

While there are many brave, courageous, clever, and skilled women in Greek myth, there are very few mortal women depicted as warriors with a similar skillset to the traditional male hero of Greek mythology. Atalanta is often seen accompanying groups of men on quests as the only female warrior in their band – consider the voyage of the Argo where she is the only female Argonaut (the name used to refer to their crew). To have an individual example of gender-non-conformity (as defined by the ancient Greeks) is not a symbol of liberation; if anything, it reinforces the patriarchal status-quo. You cannot remove the serious lack of queer women in the ancient Greek literary canon from the patriarchy that defined it.

This disconnect between the depiction of a strong woman in a world rife with female oppression is something I imagine a lot of modern women will find coming to Atalanta's story. We constantly seek out empowering stories from the past yet there is something about Atalanta's that just misses the mark – not because of Atalanta herself, but because of the context in which it was perceived at the time; she is an oddity who must eventually be forced to marry i.e. conform to the expectations of women at the time. This is something Elizabeth Tammi voiced herself. 'Reading different versions of the myth of Atalanta intrigued me as much as it confused me; I connected so viscerally with this character and I was captivated by all the other influences and challenges in her life. At the same time, I couldn't help feeling like there might be 'more' to the story happening in the background, and gradually, the reimagining of her story became *Outrun the Wind* as I added new characters and motivations. I took a ton of liberties with it, but that's what makes writing any retelling so exciting. You have to figure out for yourself what the undeniable heart of the story is, while identifying what the more fluid aspects are. It's something you can make entirely your own, but it also maintains a shared bond with all the other iterations of the story throughout history.'

As a woman in Greek myth who already defies the confines of her gender expectations, Atalanta is a perfect subject for Tammi's creative endeavour. Through following the Greek heroine's life as a complete narrative we witness the way in which people reacted to her as an outsider who behaved unlike women were expected to do, and how these same people attempted to make her better fit the role mapped out for her in society. Atalanta is a princess whose value to her people is to marry and gain a lucrative alliance for her family. As is consistent with her ancient mythological depiction, marriage is not the thing that she desires: it is a threat to her way of life. Tammi takes this further by introducing the possibility that Atalanta may have felt differently if she were allowed to marry a woman and, in establishing her romantic relationship with Kahina, she highlights the coercive actions of Hippomenes, who effectively forces himself upon Atalanta.

The introduction of Kahina meanwhile offers a parallel story of a woman quite different to Atalanta but equally stifled by the patriarchal society she inhabits. Kahina is a priestess of Apollo. She was abducted and sold by her own cousin, who, in Tammi's story, is Hippomenes, spotlighting the dangers of the slave trade in ancient Greece. She then becomes a priestess of Apollo and is given the 'gift' of prophecy. This gift is used as a metaphor for Kahina's own lack of choices. She is shimmied back and forth throughout Greece to fulfil roles others expect of her and is never asked what she wants; just as she is forced to parrot the prophecies of a god she did not choose whilst being denied her own voice.

The novel uses mythological characters and events to examine contemporary society as much as it does the ancient world. Tammi draws out the timeless stories of women who are denied their own decisions and provides them with a hopeful future in the relationship between Kahina and Atalanta. Alone, as she is in myth, Atalanta cannot escape her fate, but with the introduction of the love between herself and Kahina, the possibility of happiness is renewed. Both central characters are young women at a certain point in their life, no-longer children and on the cusp of womanhood. The concept of 'teenage years' is not one that existed in antiquity yet the young women in *Outrun the Wind* reflect that period in life as we understand it today, when many young women are discovering themselves and their sexuality, while adjusting to a world that suddenly sees them differently.

It's a wonderful example of how mythology continues to provide space for exploration to each new generation, understanding themselves and those around them.

It is important to remember that queer relationships are not only romantic ones though. As a community who all too regularly face rejection from our families and communities, like Apollo in *Midnighter and Apollo* or Raya in *Orpheus Girl*, found family is an integral part of queer culture. Literature can not only be a safe space in itself, but it can also provide models for what safe spaces look like among others. The more visible it is in media, the more people can understand what it means to us.

Maya Deane's *No Gods, No Kings* also features in the aforementioned *Fit for the Gods* (2023) anthology. Inspired in part by the mythological Titanomachy (*War of the Titans*), where the younger generation of gods known as the Olympians rebel against their forefathers and overthrow the Titan's rule, Deane chooses not to exclusively use the Greek names for the deities and figures, instead playing on the idea of mythological syncretism and the concept that the same god can have many names across cultures. Historical examples, for comparison, would be the conflation of the Celtic goddess Sulis with the Roman goddess Minerva (the latter being a goddess of wisdom so it is *assumed* that the former may have been too, but there is a lack of evidence to confirm this either way) or the Egyptian goddess Neith with the Greek goddess Athena (both verifiably goddesses of wisdom and war) by their respective cultures in antiquity.

We follow Deane's Amazonian ruler Murina as, unbeknownst to the gods, she readies her people for a rebellion. In mythology, the Amazons are an exclusive community of skilled women warriors who crop up in various stories from ancient Greece. They function as a symbolic 'other' in much of ancient Greek literature; they are deemed uncivilised, 'masculine' when they should be 'feminine', and, while their nationality differs across sources, consistently portrayed as not-Greek.

While the Amazons of Greek mythology lived in a community exclusively made up of other women, they did have sex with men. That was where their relationship started and ended. It's not hard to imagine that a large community of women also included women who loved or had sex with other women – this is true of Deane's version. Sapphic romance is casually alluded to throughout while not being the focus of the narrative. Murina, for example, often recalls the Amazon woman she once loved, but whom it appears has passed away.

This story also tackles head on the transphobic notion that only cis-women are 'women'. During a brief but important conversation between Murina and the god known as the 'Lord of the Light', the Amazon is asked this question: 'First of the Amazons, which one of your daughters was the prodigy? The one who was born a boy?' To which Murina responds, 'I forgot, the Amazons do not care about such details.' We have already been introduced to Murina's daughters, one of whom could be labelled trans, although labels are never used. The labels aren't what's important. What stands out once again is the casualness with which this reference is made. In this moment we learn that the Amazons are a community that accept all women, cis or trans.

In some ways Deane's Amazons are still the outsiders of the story. Murina may be the narrator but she and her people are treated as outsiders by the gods, subservient mortals who matter very little. In that case, we the readers are outsiders too. We sit outside the expectations of the elite, the gods whose whims rule the lives of mortals, Amazons included. Yet, they themselves are an open community, one that is accepting of all gender-identities and sexualities. I don't want to be obtuse but is this experience not something we as modern queer people can relate to? A community who strives for inclusivity while fighting against those who push them to the outskirts?

Sometimes love and acceptance are found in surprising places, and that is something epitomised classical scholar Aimee Hinds Scott's short story *The Virgin Brides* (2021). It is told from the perspective of Iphigenia, daughter of King Agamemnon and Queen Clytemnestra, who according to Greek mythology is taken from her home under the pretence of becoming the great hero Achilles' wife, but is instead sacrificed by her own father in an attempt to appease the goddess Artemis during the Trojan War. Iphigenia either dies as planned or, according to some versions, is rescued by Artemis and made immortal. Hinds Scott's version follows the former path as we meet Iphigenia now resident in the underworld, living in the house of the husband she was promised in life but only given in death: Achilles. There is no love between Iphigenia and Achilles who spends his days with his lover Patroclus, leaving Iphigenia to while away eternity. The mundanity of the afterlife is interrupted for Iphigenia, however, when Polyxena joins their household.

In ancient Greek mythology Polyxena was a Trojan princess sacrificed atop Achilles' tomb by the Greeks upon their defeat of Troy; she was specifically chosen from among the other Trojan women as a bride for Achilles in the underworld, as he had died earlier in the war. Here we have two women, one Greek, one Trojan, who never met in life but were united by their afterlives; two women who were sacrificed by men in the name of men; two women given as brides to a man they never knew or loved; but, most importantly, two women who are able to find love in each other's arms at last: 'In death, we grasp the love denied in life.' The two women are not merely companions who share a husband; they are two women who fall in love, and it is this love that is at the centre of *The Virgin Brides*.

'One of the things I love most about queer retellings is how they can embrace gentleness and reject the violence of ancient narratives, at least as overt themes,' explains Aimee Hinds Scott, when asked about her enjoyment of the form. 'For the most part, though, queer retellings approach the connections between people with a tenderness I find lacking in many non-queer receptions. There are many narratives and characters, including those well-represented in general and feminist retelling, that would benefit from this kind of tender and complex touch, and I hope to see more writers tackle them in the future.'

When I reflect, it's true that the themes touched on time and time again have been love, acceptance, and connection, whether that's because it's what I've gravitated to or that's what dominates this sub-genre – maybe it's a little bit of both. *The Virgin Brides* gives both the reader and the women of myth something neither could have found in the texts written down by and reflective of a patriarchal society that conceives of women's sexuality only in how it relates to men. As the final line reads: 'I kiss my wife. Our husband and his lover become pale shades haunting the house of Iphigenia.' These words circle back nicely to an earlier mention of 'the house of Achilles' in the story, finally offering Iphigenia the opportunity to be the main character of her own story; one about queer connection in a world that has overlooked it for too long.

Polyxena and Iphigenia's relationship is one reflected elsewhere too – I immediately think of *Stone Heart* by Katee Robert (2022), where the gorgon Medusa and nymph Callisto find an unexpected happiness with each other they were denied in their ancient stories, to name but one. And this makes me wonder, are we as queer readers and writers just as eager to give a little of the queer euphoria we experience in these novels back to the characters who inspire us? These queer myth retellings, whether the bestsellers taking the world by storm, or those singular stories capturing fragments of this history, offer new opportunities for both contemporary readers and ancient figures – opportunities to be the main character, for their stories to be treated with the complexity, depth, and tenderness that they deserve.

Conclusion

In her novel *Girl Meets Boy* (2007), a queer retelling of the Roman myth Iphis and Ianthe, Ali Smith states, 'It's what we do with the myths we grow up with that matters.' To steal from a discussion I had in my PhD thesis, myth is active. Classicist Helen Morales describes myth as being 'a process as much as a thing', something that, to understand what it is, we must consider what it does. It is living, it is breathing. When classicist Lowell Edmunds describes myth as 'a retold story about gods and heroes', the word 'retold' can be interpreted in two ways: told again or told differently. Myths are stories which are repeated but they are also stories which can be reworked, and this is as much true now as it was in antiquity. With care and respect, LGBTQIA+ writers, readers, and worshippers can and are claiming space for themselves and our community, both in these ancient stories and in today's literary world.

Mythology has and continues to offer those who appreciate it a canvas through which to explore their identity.

This book is neither the beginning nor the end of a much larger conversation. It's simply my little contribution, an attempt to chart some of what has been said so far, and a celebration of those who have been a part of it. While it can often be a solitary thing to write or read a book (she says as she sits at her desk, occasionally talking to the Bratz doll she has next to her), the sheer reach of literature makes the queering of mythology more akin to offering out a hand than locking oneself away. When chatting to queer people about this book and its subject, writers, reviewers or simply readers, every single one of them told me they had in some way connected with other readers and members of LGBTQIA+ community through these stories. Sometimes it was simply liking each other's content, while other times it was finding friends or falling in love. Maybe you bought this book because someone else mentioned it online, or you started up a conversation with a bookseller based on the title, those are connections too – whether fleeting or forever, each of these connections are important to remember when looking at a subject such as this.

From epic poetry to fantasy romance, queer Greek myth retellings come in many different shapes and forms. As has been evident since antiquity, mythology is ever-evolving, but no matter the guise or shape it takes, its recognisability is also what provides that stage upon which to act out new versions. It is both of these things, the malleability and the familiarity, that offer a haven for modern queer folk to explore those timeless emotions and experiences that feel so personal, how the LGBTQIA+ community, my community, has found such a profound connection through these tales. Because, as Kae Tempest's *Brand New Ancients* aptly puts it: 'All that we have here is all that we've always had.'

Throughout this book, LGBTQIA+ writers and readers have reclaimed an ancient and timeless form of storytelling. These writers have reimagined recognisable characters and stories to give voice to a community that has always existed but has not always been able to speak out. There is something incredibly powerful in taking stories so timeless, retold by so many and for so long, and creating the space for queer identity to flourish within it. To say, *hey, we belong here as much as anyone.* Queering the Greek myths is simultaneously an act of rebellion and an act that honours the legacy of these remarkable stories. Like Pandora's jar, these are most often filled with hope; struggle, yes, grief, yes, but in the end, hope is found at the bottom of the vessel. Together our community has carved out a safe space in the transformed versions of these myths and found connection through them; connection to ourselves, to each other, to the past, and to the future. So, whatever the reason, whatever my reason, whatever yours – here we are queering the Greek Myths.

If you're interested in finding more Greek (and Roman) myth retellings, queer or not, I have compiled an (incomplete but ever expanding) database over on my website you might find useful:

www.jeanmenzies.com/myth-retellings-database

References

1   It is worth noting that the subject of classics is an academic construct with a long history but one which continues to be redefined and reconstructed as new scholars and enthusiasts join the conversation.

2   See for example: *Law, sexuality and society: the enforcement of morals in classical Athens* by David Cohen (1991); *Bisexuality in the Ancient World* by Eva Cantarella (2002); *The Greeks and Greek Love* by J. Davidson (2007); *Gender: Antiquity and Its Legacy* by Brooke Holmes (2011) & *Sex: Antiquity and Its Legacy* by Daniel Orrells (2015).

3   You can read my entire thesis on 'The Politicisation of Sexual Assault in 4th Century Athens' online via the Roehampton university research database: pure.roehampton.ac.uk/portal/en/studentTheses/the-politicisation-of-sexual-assault-in-fourth-century-athens.

4   See for example Apollodorus' *Library of Greek Mythology 3.6, and* Hyginus' *Fabulae* 75.

5   "Kae Tempest: 'I was living with this boiling hot secret in my heart'." Michael Seagalov, *The Guardian*, 12 March 2022. theguardian.com/culture/2022/mar/12/kae-tempest-i-was-living-with-this-boiling-hot-secret-in-my-heart. Accessed 22 November 2023.

6   See Apollodorus' *Library of Greek Mythology* 1.38.

7   reddit.com/r/SapphoAndHerFriend/

8   "Re-Queering Sappho." Ella Haselswerdt, *Medium*, 8 August 2016. eidolon.pub/re-queering-sappho-c6c05b6b9f0b. Accessed 22 November 2023.

9   See for example Hesiod's *Theogony* 287*ff*, Stesichorus' *Geryoneis*, and Apollodorus' *Library of Greek Mythology* 2.106*ff*.

10 "An Interview with Anne Carson." Eleanor Wachtel, *Brick*. brickmag.com/an-interview-with-anne-carson/. Accessed 22 November 2023.

11 See for example Apollodorus' *Library of Greek Mythology* 1.3*ff*, and Ovid's *Metamorphoses* 10.1-39.

12 See: legislation.gov.uk/ukpga/1988/9/section/28/enacted.

13 See *Self-Definition, Community and Resistance: Euripides' "Medea" and Toni Morrison's "Beloved"* by Shelley P. Haley, published in *Thamyris* Vol. 2 (1995).

14 See for example: gov.uk/government/publications/the-prevalence-of-conversion-therapy-in-the-uk/the-prevalence-of-conversion-therapy-in-the-uk & williamsinstitute.law.ucla.edu/press/lgb-suicide-ct-press-release.

15 dc.fandom.com/wiki/LGBT#Early_History.

16 See for example Apollodorus' *Library of Greek Mythology* 3.116*ff*, Pausanias' *Geography of Greece* 3.19.5, Lucian's *Dialogue of the Gods* 16, and Ovid's *Metamorphoses* 10.162*ff*.

17 For a discussion of the Orphic themes in *Théo et Hugo dans le même batea*u see *The Anti-Orpheus: Queering Myth in Ducastel et Martineau's Théo et Hugo dans le même bateau (Paris 05:59)* by Todd W. Reeser, published in Studies in 20th & 21st Century Literature Vol. 42 (2018).

18 "Kalynn Bayron talks about her love of horror and the need for inclusivity." Matthew Todd, *The Bookseller*, 4 April 2022. thebookseller.com/author-interviews/kalynn-bayron-talks-about-her-love-of-horror-and-the-need-for-inclusivity. Accessed 22 November 2023.

19 "Interview With Author Kalynn Bayron." Michele Kirichanskaya, *Geeks Out*, 23 July 2021. geeksout.org/2021/07/23/interview-with-author-kalynn-bayron/. Accessed 22 November 2023.

20   See for example Homer's *Iliad* 24.25–30, Apollodorus'
    Library of Greek Mythology 3.2ff, *and* Hyginus' *Fabulae* 92.
21   boxofficemojo.com/release/rl3698820609/.
22   "Phoenicia Rogerson | HERC." Ed Fortune, *Starburst*.
    https://www.starburstmagazine.com/features/phoenicia-roger-
    son-herc/. Accessed 22 November 2023.
23   Zuckerberg (2019), 150.
24   Zuckerberg (2019), 149.
25   tiktok.com/ZGJnhRmtf/
26   "The New White Nationalism's Sloppy Use of Art His-
    tory, Decoded." Ben Davis, *Artnet*, 7 March 2017. news.
    artnet.com/art-world/identity-evropa-posters-art-symbol-
    ism-881747. Accessed 22 November 2023.

About the Author

Jean Menzies is an author, ancient historian, presenter, and wannabe-dragon. In 2022 she received her PhD in classics from Roehampton University and has dedicated her career to making these topics accessible to all. Her first book *Greek Myths: Meet the heroes gods and monsters of ancient Greece* won the BAMB Breakthrough Author award in 2020 and she has since written on mythology and history for all ages. You can also find her online at @jeansthoughts pretty much anywhere, creating content about myth, history, literature, and, sometimes, board games.